BY PERLA LICHI

I am proud to say that my signature style is now sought after around the world. As my interior design practice has expanded internationally, I have designed homes for people from all walks of life -- from the regular business person to the royal prince and princess. And one thing of which I am certain is this: every man and woman wants to be king and queen of their own palace.

So my fourth book is dedicated to showing readers the gamut of possibilities for their own personal palace, and to help them visualize the magic and grandeur that is within their reach.

There are many differences in people's style preference. This book showcases rich, palatial, classical detailing -- which is my signature look -- to sleek contemporary, which is the forte of my U.S. partner, Steven Zelman. No matter which type of decor they select, however, I have discovered that people all really want the same thing. And that is a comfortable, yet elegant, and beautifully put together style that they can enjoy in health with their families. My ultimate passion is interior design because I know that people will be living in these spaces that we design and enjoying them every day of their lives. I hope you enjoy my new book.

~Perla Lichi

Perla Lichi Photo: Barry Grossman

Copyright © 2012 by
Perla Lichi LLC
www.perlalichi.com

All rights reserved. No part of this book may be reproduced in any form without prior written permission of the copyright owner. All images in the book have been reproduced with the knowledge and prior consent of the home owners, builders, artists and photographers concerned and no responsibility is accepted by the producer, publisher, distributor or printer for any infringement of copyright or otherwise arising from the contents of the publication. Every effort has been made to ensure that credits accurately comply with information supplied.

Cover Photo: Naim Chidiac

Palaces by Perla Lichi
Copyright 2012 © Perla Lichi
Perla Lichi LLC

ISBN 978-0-9851844-2-1

Trade Paperback
Published by Granny Apple Publishing LLC
Sarasota, Florida USA
www.grannyapplepublishing.com

Palaces
BY PERLA LICHI

Editor & Publisher Janet Verdeguer
Graphic Designer Miguel Valcarcel

Photographer Naim Chidiac
Photographer Barry Grossman
Photographer Salamaat Husain

Published February 2012 by
Granny Apple Publishing LLC

FOREWORD

Presented in this book are photographs of ten recently designed luxury palaces, each one extraordinary in its own way:

❧ *The Regal Palace, with its fresh palette of rich gold and aquamarine and silver-leafed columns with bronze detailing.*

❧ *The Winter Palace with its custom, handcarved furniture, special finishes and magnificent draperies made of luscious fabrics.*

❧ *The Grand Palace, which combines Tuscan, Mediterranean and Moorish styles into an elegant, warm and inviting ambiance.*

❧ *The Spring Palace's amazing finishes including metallic copper leaf and crocodile skin finished in pewter.*

❧ *The 21st Century Palace with its 24-foot coffered ceiling supported with floor-to-ceiling contemporary columns finished in glossy white.*

As you enjoy looking through all of these unique palaces, each with a distinct flavor, you may find yourself drawn to a particular one. You will probably see elements in some or all of them that you particularly like.

When you are ready to build or remodel, we can use these photographs to provide a reference point so that we know exactly how to proceed to bring your own very personal design dreams to life. Then you, too, will be king and queen of your own palace. I can't wait!

~ Perla Lichi

Contents

The Regal Palace
Dubai, UAE
11 - 24

The Imperial Palace
Abu Dhabi, UAE
25-57

The Spring Palace
Abu Dhabi, UAE
59-79

The Summer Palace
Dubai, UAE
81-100

Contents

The Autumn Palace
THE PALM, Dubai, UAE
101-114

The Winter Palace
Dubai, UAE
115-126

The Majestic Palace
Sharjah, UAE
127-146

Contents

The Grand Palace
Fort Lauderdale, Florida USA
147-166

The Chic Palace
Dubai, UAE
167-182

The 21st Century Palace
Lichi-Zelman Style Interiors
Boca Raton, Florida USA
183-200

REGAL PALACE

Dubai, UAE

Photography by Salamaat Husain

Palaces ~ 17

Imperial Palace

Abu Dhabi, UAE

Photography by Naim Chidiac

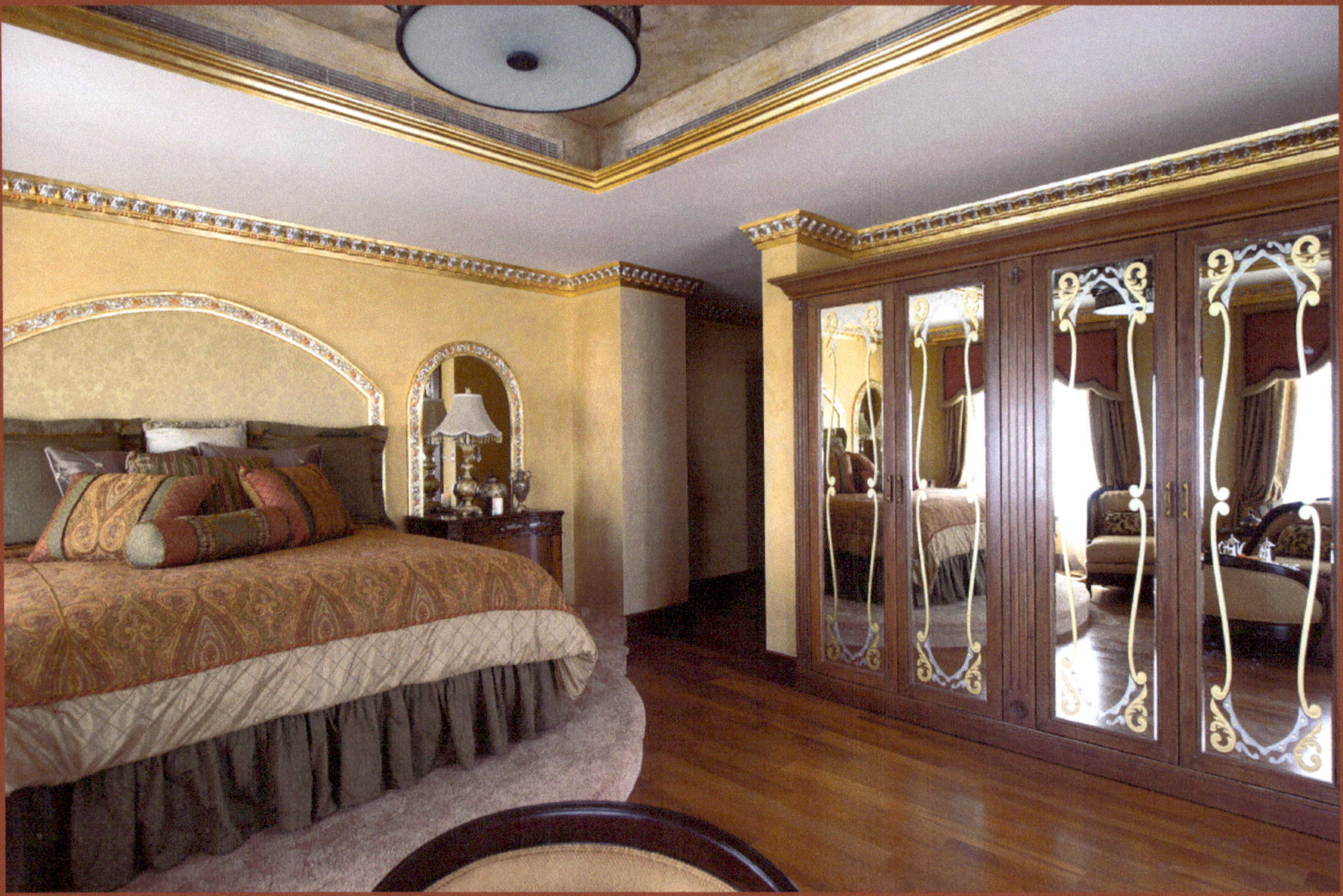

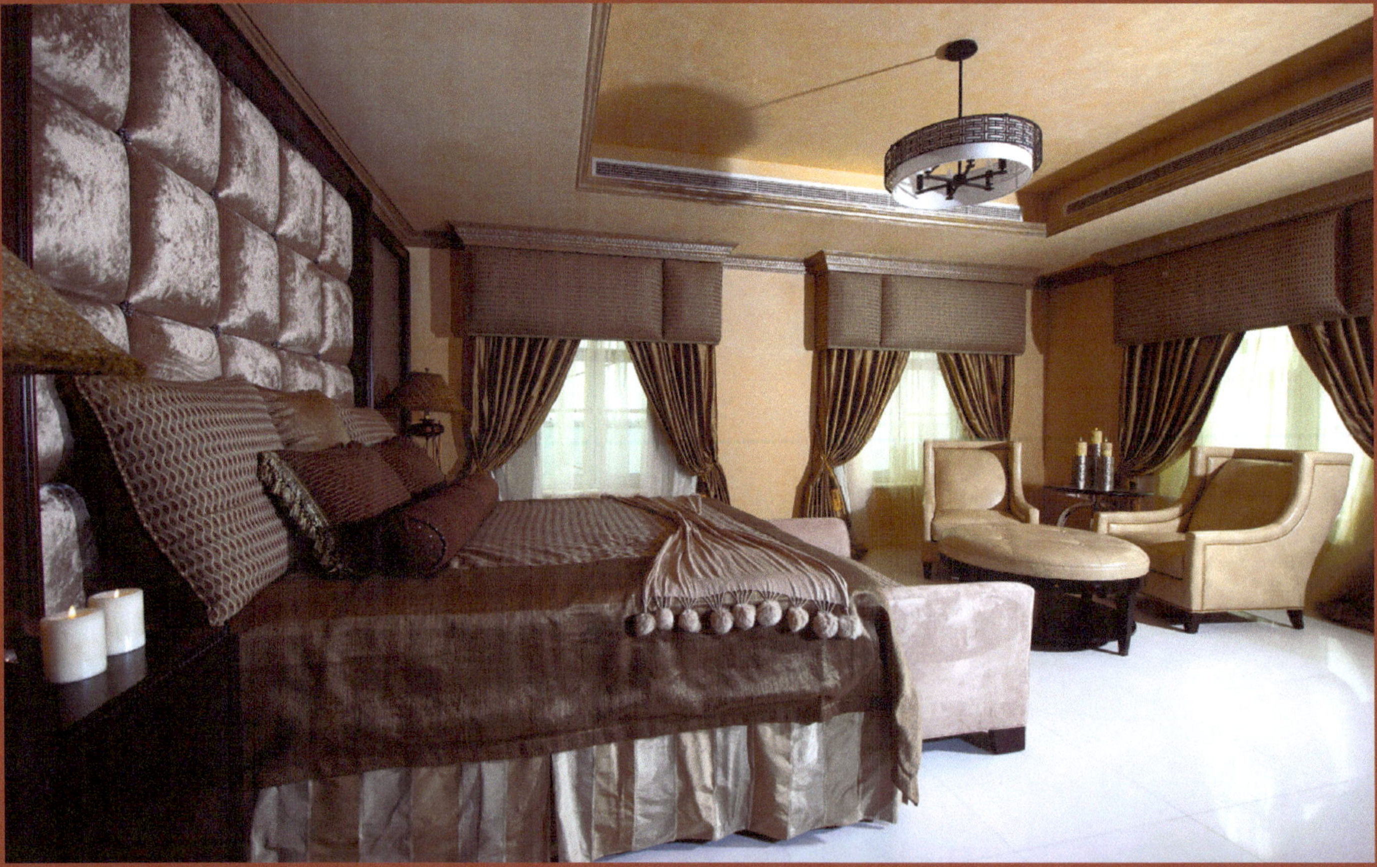

Palaces ~ 47

Spring Palace

Abu Dhabi, UAE

Photography by Naim Chidiac

Palaces ~ 73

Summer Palace

Abu Dhabi, UAE

Photography by Naim Chidiac

     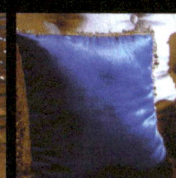

Palaces ~ 89

Autumn Palace

The Palm, Dubai

Photography by Naim Chidiac

Palaces ~ 105

Palaces ~ 107

Winter Palace

Perla Lichi Gallery

Photography by Salamaat Husain

Palaces ~ 123

Majestic Palace

Sharjah, UAE

Photography by Naim Chidiac

Palaces ~ **139**

Grand Palace

Fort Lauderdale, Florida

Photography by Barry Grossman

Palaces ~ **165**

Chic PALACE

Burj Dubai, Dubai UAE

Photography by Naim Chidiac

Palaces ~ 171

Palaces ~ 175

Palaces ~ 179

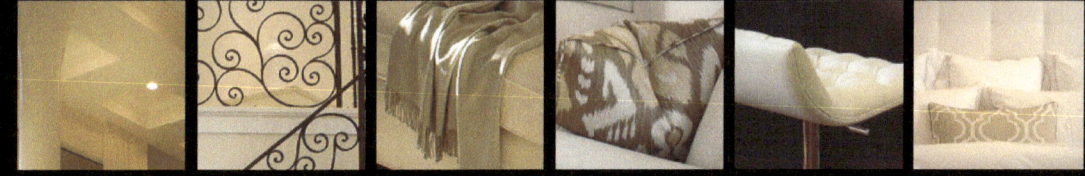

21st Century Palace

Boca Raton, Florida

Photography by Barry Grossman

Interior Design Renovation
by Steven Zelman
of Lichi-Zelman Style Interiors

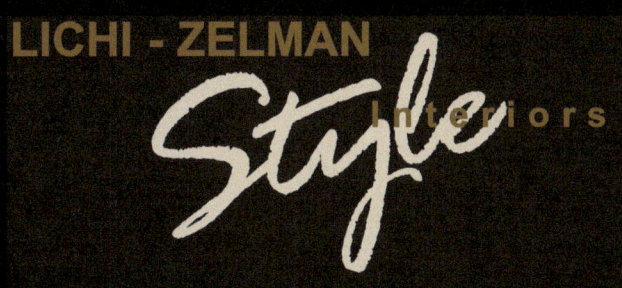

Palaces ~ *193*

Palaces ~ **199**

About Perla Lichi

Perla Lichi, ASID, has become a major force in the US and International interior design communities. She has seen her namesake design firm grow from local strength to national and international prominence and is currently working on residential projects across the USA and around the globe.

Born in Mexico and educated in the United States, this globe-trotting designer is constantly sought out by the world's most successful people who want her unique design talents to enhance their homes and lifestyles. Since founding her namesake firm in Florida in 1990, Perla Lichi has enjoyed great success in high-end residential design. Her clients have included royalty, successful entrepreneurs, business executives and professionals in every field including sports.

She brings to her profession passion, talent and enthusiasm and takes a hands-on approach with every client who commissions her. Perla is a creative, innovative designer with sound business sense. She is also a specialist in art history, color, and space planning, with a keen eye for detail and architectural elements. Her firm excels at providing custom design for every element of the interior, from start to finish.

Perla Lichi
Perla Lichi LLC, Parkland, FL
877-716-1563
www.perlalichi.com

Palaces by Perla Lichi
Copyright © 2012 Perla Lichi

ISBN 978-0-9851844-2-1

Published by Granny Apple Publishing, LLC
Sarasota, FL

www.ingramcontent.com/pod-product-compliance
Lightning Source LLC
Chambersburg PA
CBHW041024040526
R18239800001B/R182398PG44116CBX00001B/1